Child Welfare League of America, Inc.

The ABCs of Child Care Work in Residential Care

THE LINDEN HILL MANUAL

Paul Lambert

Current printing (last digit):

10 9 8 7 6 5 4 3

Library of Congress Catalog Card Number: 77-73022
ISBN: 0-87868-165-5

Contents

Foreword

Although we frequently profess that our children are the
nation's most valuable asset and precious resource, we
have used them badly, especially the fragile, the disturbed
and the handicapped. This manual is an attempt to
describe a basic approach to the care of atypical children,
particularly in the day-to-day living so crucial to their
growth and development.

In recent years and in many places, child care has been
moving from vocation to profession. In the early years of
residential treatment, the child care worker was viewed
narrowly as a surrogate parent, whose role and
qualifications were essentially domestic. But if the child
care workers or cottage couples were "typical," the
children were not, and more often than not we were not
able to bridge the gap between the cottage and the clinic.

Today, there is increasing deemphasis on the parental
role in favor of a trained professional approach to the child
care task and a parity, so to speak, between the formal
treatment hour and the daily living experience of the child.
Child care still remains a vocation, albeit in the best sense,

but it is increasingly recognized as a specialty that requires a higher education and training.

This recognition of the need to professionalize the total child care task has opened up new career opportunities. Not only have inservice training programs been accelerated and broadened in most child caring facilities, but the child care curriculum is being installed in both community and 4-year colleges.

This is a signal advance, although all the problems are far from solved. We look forward with hope to the meaningful impact that the professionalization of the child care task can have on the lives of atypical children.

Jerome M. Goldsmith, Ed.D.
Executive Vice President
Jewish Board of Guardians

Introduction

This manual for child care workers was originally developed to achieve consistency in our child care program and it is thus specifically tailored for Linden Hill School. Requests from other institutions for copies of the manual were so frequent that we decided to make it more widely available. To further its general applicability, some portions have been rewritten and the daily chronology of routines has been omitted. The reader should derive from the manual a philosophy about the care of children.

Our own attitude toward the treatment of adolescents was forged in 1953, when Linden Hill School opened. The Jewish Board of Guardians, of which Linden Hill is a division, has for more than 80 years been devoted to the inpatient and outpatient treatment of emotionally disturbed children. The agency had long recognized that a great need existed for a therapeutic setting for the confused, bizarre and difficult-to-manage adolescents who, at that time, had only state hospitals available to them. A program was designed in which people, not bars and locked doors, would be in control. Such a program, of necessity, requires clarity and consistency in its objectives. Consequently, the manual is a useful tool in orienting new child care workers and for referral to as particular issues arise.

The Linden Hill School is situated in Westchester County, about 35 miles from New York City. It is a residential treatment center for severely disturbed adolescent boys and girls from the ages of 12 to 16 who require and can use intensive treatment in an open setting, individual and family therapy, a variety of group therapies, group living and an educational program. It has capacity for 33 boys and 22 girls in its main building. In addition, eight children who are advanced in treatment live off-grounds in nearby Ossining, in a house that is an annex of the main institution.

On-grounds, Linden Hill consists of two buildings. One is a modern plant that includes living quarters for children and child care staff, an infirmary, administrative and clinic offices, and facilities for research. The second, older building, which formerly housed the entire Linden Hill program, is now used for the academic program. The grounds are unfenced and the entrance doors of the residence are never locked. The children's living quarters consist of five apartments, each housing 11 children, two for the girls and three for the boys. Each apartment has a living room, kitchen, dining room and single and double bedrooms. The apartments are designed to provide a family-like atmosphere.

The Linden Hill Program

Child Care

A high ratio, approximately 1 to 2, of staff to children makes possible direct and continuous supervision of the children in their daily nonacademic life. The work of this staff is closely coordinated with that of other departments through frequent case conferences, staff meetings and supervisory conferences. Staff members on duty at all times provide supervision of the children 24 hours a day. The relationships between the children and the child care staff are a crucial aspect of the total treatment program. The child care staff is responsible for the development of defined standards of living and for the children's adherence to them.

To the extent that individual children can benefit, activities and trips in the community are planned. These take place with staff supervision or, where possible, without such supervision, and include shopping expeditions, medical and educational appointments, recreation, Y membership meetings, paid and volunteer employment, and regular home visits.

Big Brother and Big Sister volunteers help the children develop and profit from relationships and experiences outside the institution. Professional staff supervise volunteers to integrate their work with the overall program.

Clinical Services

The clinical staff consists of a psychiatrist who is the clinical director, three part-time psychiatrists, two psychologists, six psychiatric caseworkers (one of whom is a casework supervisor), and a chief psychiatric social worker. The clinical staff is responsible for intake evaluation, individual and group treatment, psychological testing, and followup after discharge. The staff also conducts a long-term research program on certain aspects of institutionalization as a treatment and observation tool.

Treatment begins at the moment of the child's admission to Linden Hill and consists mainly of individual and group therapy for the children. In addition, family group therapy sessions, meetings with parent groups on immediate problems, and visits by the therapist to the family home are continually emphasized. In day-to-day functioning, emphasis is placed on exchange of information among clinical administrators, child care workers and educational staff, with reports from parents incorporated in the general thinking and program planning for the youngster.

Medication is used when indicated for specific emotional

and behavioral symptoms. Our philosophy is to use it only selectively and sparingly, and for limited periods of time, with the expectation that most, if not all, of the youngsters will manage eventually without any medication.

Education

Specialized education, from primary to 12th grade, is provided by the Hawthorne Cedar Knolls Union Free School District. Linden Hill children attend classes in their own school building. Because most of our children are underachievers or have special learning difficulties, remedial instruction plays a large part in the educational program.

Each Linden Hill child has a program tailored to his educational needs and attends school for the full day. Teaching is done mainly in small class units; some individual instruction is given in mathematics and reading. The school grants 8th- and 9th-grade diplomas and can prepare children for state regents examinations for high school diplomas. A major objective of the educational program is the preparation of the child for a return to his proper grade level in the community school system. With this in mind, the school provides an academic curriculum within a regular school framework.

Medical and Dental Services

An infirmary under the supervision of two part-time pediatricians and two full-time registered nurses provides, among other services, medical evaluation procedures that take into account not only the illness itself and the altering of the child's physical status, but an understanding of how a specific medical procedure will be viewed and accepted by the child, and will fit into his total institutional experience. The physician and nurse consult the psychiatrist, caseworkers and administrative personnel, thus becoming part of the residential treatment team. A part-time dentist is available for routine examination and treatment, and his service is likewise integrated into the total treatment program.

Acknowledgments

This manual would never have been written without the contributions of many individuals who helped to shape its contents. I would like to express my appreciation of all the help they have given over the years.

Paul Lambert
Director
Linden Hill School

Child Care Fundamentals

Teamwork Among Child Care Workers

Teamwork among child care workers is essential for several reasons. It is best for children to have as consistent an approach and method of handling as possible. Children tend to manipulate by playing one child care worker against the other. Consequently, child care workers gain a mutual feeling of support from the knowledge that a decision will be carried out by coworkers. This holds not only for the time the child care worker is on duty, but during his absence. The children gain a sense of continuity in the staff, and their attempts to break down structure are minimized. Actually, the children want the structure maintained for their own safety and well-being.

The child care worker has greater freedom of action when he can rely on other child care workers to back him up and work with him in carrying out agreed practices. The ideal team approach is achieved when two child care workers, working together, recognize that they must maintain the structure of the living situation consistently, but yet know that they each retain freedom of action in other areas.

A basic ingredient of good teamwork is communication. Any out-of-the-ordinary decision made by a child care worker is to be communicated to the other at the earliest moment. Many brief conferences are usually necessary during the course of a day. A new approach that a child care worker plans to use can be worked out in such a conference. If a child is upset, this should be communicated quickly, even though the child care worker is handling the child satisfactorily. The reason for this is that there may be repercussions later from the child or the group.

When child care workers disagree on what action to take, they must realize that a decision has to be made and that both must support it fully. Differences can be ironed out later or taken to the supervisor. A united front must be presented to the child at all times.

Contradiction of one staff member by another in front of the children is to be avoided. If it is necessary to discuss with a child care worker a possible misstatement or wrong action, it is always preferable to take him aside and present the other point of view. Each child care worker must be aware of the routine schedule of activities such as snacks, laundry and cleanup and take a hand in planning and carrying them out. Each must know what is going on and the part the other child care worker is playing so that each can give support to the other. Cooperative support can be achieved in two ways: one, by actively working with the other child care worker, and two, by seeing that the routine goes on according to schedule. Any group meeting with the children should involve both child care workers, whenever possible. Also, mutual support is necessary to pull reluctant children into the meeting.

Whenever a child care worker decides to leave the building while he is on duty, or to take children away for an activity, he should notify his coworker. The child care worker should consider the number of children that are left behind during his absence as well as the general atmosphere prevailing in the building at the time. A feeling of mutual confidence is created when each child care worker is constantly aware of his responsibility not only to the individual child but to the group as a whole.

Teamwork among child care workers of the various units in the facility is necessary to achieve interunit cooperation. The child care worker should be aware of the atmosphere and the behavior of the children in other units. At times of stress, feelings are contagious and easily spark similar behavior in other units. Action taken in one unit frequently creates a sympathetic reaction in another. The child care worker supports the action taken in the other unit and sees that his children do not interfere. There are times when it is necessary to call a child care worker from another unit for assistance. The child care worker calling for assistance should not look upon this action as evidence of failure; rather, he should feel secure in knowing that he can expect the support and cooperation needed.

Since our children are constantly socializing, it is necessary that the boys' and girls' child care workers keep each other apprised of boy-girl relationships and any other factors that might affect the children in general. Knowledge of any unusual behavior among the children should be shared, including concern that some untoward activity is in the wind.

If a child care worker feels that his coworker is not functioning properly, or is making errors in judgment, he should discuss this with the worker concerned, and later, with the supervisor. Matters of this kind should not be allowed to stew; if they are, they definitely will interfere with work. Anything affecting harmonious relationships between counselors creates an atmosphere of nonsupport that is frequently sensed by the children. Therefore, discord of any kind and for any reason should be cleared up as soon as practicable. This is the child care worker's professional responsibility, since an effective job cannot be done if disharmony exists.

Teamwork enables child care workers to feel that responsibility is being shouldered equally. The stresses and strains inherent in work with children should not be increased by the added tensions of poor staff relationships.

Attitudes of the Child Care Worker

The child care worker's primary objective is simple: to help children face a set of new interpersonal experiences. To accomplish this end, patience and understanding of the youngsters' odd behavior and distorted values are among the most valuable personal qualities a child care worker can have. Maintaining an adult relationship with the children and being able to control overidentification enhance the child care worker's attainment of this goal. The job calls for the child care worker to be consistent, convincing and interested, and to communicate strength, fairness and kindness to the child. All possible control is needed against projection of our own feelings onto the child. We should not overemphasize a personal value by standing in moral judgment of the child's behavior. A course of action is determined by what we think will help a child to get along with people in accordance with a predetermined treatment plan.

Characteristically, some children relate with inappropriate love and hate. At times a staff member is treated as a child's beloved defender and later (often in a matter of minutes), as a source of all the youngster's frustration, rejection and disappointments. Knowledge of the child should help the child care worker deal with inappropriate emotions by objectifying them and impersonalizing them.

Members of the child care staff possess a diversity of life experiences stemming not only from the differences in age and sex, but from their highly individual family and educational backgrounds. Consequently, each child care worker comes to the job with a unique point of view. The biographical variations almost guarantee the likelihood that attitudes will not be the same about a number of issues.

It is hoped that the highly personal approaches taken by

child care workers toward the children are not so disparate as to cause severe disagreement between coworkers or between workers and the program. Since the society in an institution is not very different from that in the outside world, it is necessary to watch out for attitudes that do not quite fit into the program and that clash with those of other staff members.

What Are Some of These Problems?

Let us take *cleanliness* as an example. It is a matter in which attitudes are important because of the different reactions it provokes in each child care worker. Striving for standards of cleanliness is a necessary objective. At the same time, a child care worker must be able to accept the prevailing level of functioning of the individual child. Extremes of over- or under-expectation seriously hamper the opportunity the child care worker has to help a child and may hinder desirable change. In short, the child care worker's objective is to create a balance between what the child must do and what he is able to do, without sacrificing the objectives of the program.

Overall standards of cleanliness are expected to be met by the entire student body. The standard may be above or below the child care worker's own expectation. Further, expectation based on a child's individual abilities, differing even temporarily from overall standards, is sometimes difficult for the child care worker to accept. In consequence, a lack of sensitivity on the part of the child care worker to the fine balance between flexibility and inflexibility can cause friction with coworkers and confuse the child as well.

One's personal example of cleanliness is important; how we dress reflects an attitude that is quickly picked up by children. By virtue of our role and relationship we become objects with whom children tend to identify. Consequently, extra care should be used in regard to personal appearance, as well as conduct.

It should be clear that going on duty is the same as *going to work.* At first, a child care worker may find it difficult to make a sharp distinction between job and home situations. The difficulty may arise because of the agency's emphasis on "family atmosphere." The effort to keep the distinction clear is especially needed when child care workers live in the same building as the children. Without doubt, living in the residence produces a special attitude toward the job; it seems more relaxed and informal.

A child care worker's failure to distinguish carefully between a *sense of humor*, on the one hand, and "kidding around," sarcasm, teasing and horseplay, on the other, contributes to disagreement among coworkers. The former can be of great help in undercutting a child's provocation, and useful in many other ways, while the latter can only have the negative effect of stimulating a child to become unmanageable, or result in behavior that requires disciplinary measures. Experience has taught child care workers to avoid disparagement: sarcasm ("Well, you look like you lost your last friend"); name calling (Shorty, Fatty, Pinhead, etc.); and dire prediction ("You won't ever grow up!"). Also, calling children by their last names sounds disrespectful. Can there be any disagreement over calling children by their first names?

Like other children, ours invest strong feelings in the significant persons who enter their lives: child care workers, therapists, teachers (as examples among staff), parents, siblings, and other relatives in the family constellation. All make easy targets for the expression of love and hate. In interaction with the children, the child care worker must be careful of his *attitudes toward others.* Children latch onto negative feelings expressed by one staff member toward another, and often use the statements to the detriment of the workers. Jealousies, prejudices and personal frustrations that a child care worker feels about another staff member should be discussed with his supervisor. In any event, talk in the children's presence about the qualities of other staff members, or the child care worker's own problems with administration, tends to feed the children's dissatisfaction and need to manipulate. The more such talk there is, the greater will be the dysfunction between child care workers and children. Attitudes toward other staff and administration should be supportive of their roles and functions.

Child care workers should consider carefully their use of *language patterns.* What does a child learn from them?

14

For instance, when it seems suitable, answering "You decide," or "Whatever you want," rather than "Yes," helps a child learn to operate on his own initiative, not just to take orders. Another example: "The light is on in your room" is better than "Turn the light out in your room."

Accountability and Responsibility

It behooves the child care worker to know where his children are at all times. That adults want to know where their children are conveys a sense of caring and security. Children, at bottom, want adults to be concerned about their physical well-being and their whereabouts. Otherwise, children show anxiety because they don't know what to expect from adults, and they frequently act out their uncertainty.

The child care worker should always keep in mind the whereabouts of the children he is responsible for, checking his knowledge every 15 minutes or so; if he is doubtful about a youngster's whereabouts, he should look for him. Some may consider this procedure "snooping" or excessive worry, but it pays off. Locating the youngster and saying "I wondered how you are" or some other caring phrase will transmit the appropriate concern.

If permission is to be given to go off grounds, a preparatory discussion with the child should take place. Where, how long, what the youngster will be doing, if he has enough money, transportation problems, phone number if visiting someone, etc., are pertinent points to cover. The youngster should be held to the agreed time of return and excuses for lateness should not be readily

15

accepted. The child care worker should express not only disappointment but concern. The child care worker should remember the tardiness and remind the youngster when discussing a future trip off grounds.

Frequently, child care workers who begin to be firm and consistent in implementing accountability are surprised at the positive response they receive from children. Those children who seemed most unlikely to accept adult interest will, after a while, come on their own to let their child care workers know where they are going.

Responsibility goes hand in hand with accountability. Responsibility here means the recognition that a person must accept the consequences of his behavior. The idea that a child is responsible for his actions runs throughout this manual. If a child is responsible for his personal property, he is also responsible for the property of others, both private and public. If a child borrows an item from another child, the child is responsible for returning it in the same condition as received. For this reason, it is always good practice for the child care worker to involve himself in or at least be aware of lending and borrowing among children. Parenthetically, this applies to other exchanges of articles by swapping or purchase. Child care workers should make known to the group that they want to know about such transactions to prevent one child from exploiting another. It is true that it is difficult, especially with adolescents, to keep abreast of all the lending that goes on, but at the very least, the worker should make the ground rules explicitly understood.

With regard to public property, the rule of thumb is "If you break it, you pay for it." Because somebody has to pay for the damage, it should be the person who did it. Since the breaking of furniture, windows and equipment, the marking of walls with grafitti and other acts of destruction are often vehicles for the expression of anger, the child care worker must have a clearly defined approach to convey to the child or children. No distinction should be made between willful and malicious acts of destruction and damage due to temper tantrums or other outbursts of rage, but a distinction should be made as to accidental causes of damage. In doing so, the child care worker must decide whether the damage was really accidental or whether that assertion is just an excuse to avoid responsibility. It is an invalid excuse when two youngsters break something while horsing around and then say the breakage was accidental.

In the face of nonaccidental destruction, the child care worker must recognize the anger as a legitimate, highly personal feeling that the child has a right to have. Being angry is one thing, but how the anger is expressed is another. The child care worker should not confuse the two features of an act of destruction and should handle them separately. Accordingly, the child care worker must not excuse the destruction or mutilation of property belonging to others. In the process of arranging how the child will pay for the damage caused, the child care worker can explain to the child socially acceptable ways of expressing anger that would avoid the problem of restitution.

Payment for the damaged or broken property should not be seen as punishment, but as a way of teaching that a reaction can be expected to every action. If the manner in which the child care worker presents the consequences is perceived as punishment, the lesson is lost. The method of repayment, however expensive the damage, must be worked out without overwhelming the child. He can repay by deductions made from his allowance, and he can be offered the opportunity to do paid work to facilitate payment of the debt.

Meaning of Chores and Work

Doing chores is an essential part of the milieu treatment. Children should share the experience in community living that can be achieved through chores. It is not just a matter of getting the job done, or keeping the living area "clean." Attitudes toward the assignment and toward working with others, as well as learning skills, are the important part of this function.

Child care workers should use chores to help children learn to work together and to impose a sense of responsibility — community as well as individual. The youngster will get a feeling of belonging in a system of relationships when he feels he is making a worthwhile contribution. In addition, chores offer an opportunity to develop a positive attitude toward work and gain a sense of satisfaction from it. The best way to teach a child is to work along with him and show him what to do and how to do it. The child care worker thus becomes an enabler and teacher — there is no room for a maid or butler or straw boss. If the child sees that the chore is important to the child care worker, he will become more aware of the need to do it and will express more positive feeling toward the job. If it is felt that a child can do a better job than he has done, the child care worker can insist that he do the chore over again until he does it to the best of his ability.

Since chores are a part of social and group living, they must be carried out. Each time a child is allowed to avoid his assigned chore, he is being cheated of the total effectiveness of the milieu treatment program.

The work planned for a child is always within his emotional and physical capacity; it is never beyond his strength and endurance. Child care workers soon learn that children will readily pick up whatever conflict or uncertainty the staff may have about the job to be done, or about children working. The child care worker's indecisiveness will create critical situations that will turn into a power struggle between the child and the child care worker: "Let me see you make me!"

In summary, respect for work can be conveyed to children only if adults around them have a respect for it themselves and express it in terms of action, not by lip service. The work habits of children are influenced by the child care worker's attitude, which is reflected in his own punctuality, attendance and effort. If an adult exploits others to accomplish what he himself should do, he is doing a disservice to the positive aspect of work.

Confidentiality

When a child comes into the institution, his life is unavoidably an open book to everyone, staff and children alike. The issue of confidentiality is sharpest when knowledge of the child's placement and his history goes beyond the "walls" of the institution. Every child has the right to privacy, and child care staff, as well as others, must respect this right.

Child care workers can violate the right of a child to privacy in a number of ways. A child care worker may see a name he recognizes or an address he is familiar with — that of the child of a friend or relative or neighbor — and thoughtlessly inquire as to the connection. The child care worker should not go to someone else on staff and say, "Do you know that so-and-so's child is with us?" Conversely, it may happen that a friend or relative of the child care worker may know that so-and-so's child is in the institution, and ask how he is doing. In this situation, the child care worker must be noncommittal. In other instances, he should admit to no one that a particular child is in placement.

Talking about "cases" at private gatherings away from the institution also violates confidentiality. The concerns and fears of the child care worker about certain children should be avoided as topics of conversation. Names or other identifying information should not be divulged.

Within the institution, the issue of confidentiality takes on a different quality and can sometimes be confusing. For example, when a child says, "I'll tell you something if you promise not to tell anyone," this seemingly puts the child care worker in a spot. The child care worker has to make the distinction between "secrets" and confidential information. Too, youngsters frequently make such requests because they really want the staff to know, and the child care worker should not obscure the issue by withholding the information from other staff members who ought to be informed.

Again, staff should not talk to children about other children. Also, child care workers should be on their guard never to talk with another staff member about a child within earshot of extraneous adults or other children.

Interpretation of Rules

Rules! Rules! Rules! No matter where the child care worker turns, there seems to be some rule that must be observed — so many do's and don't's that the child care worker is often confused about which takes precedence over another. If the child care worker is confused, imagine how the youngster must feel!

Like taxes, rules are here to stay, and it behooves the child care worker to learn as much as he can about them. Rules define the structure within which both the child care worker and the child must live. Without rules, there would be chaos; there can be no program, and the children cannot be treated properly. Although each rule has a reason, not all rules have the same priority. The seemingly arbitrary rules are most troublesome, and most difficult to interpret to the children.

Rules are made to protect the integrity of a program, and represent also expectations of behavior, but they must not be relied upon to explain themselves. The child care worker has a responsibility for explaining rules. It is not enough to answer a child's "why?" with "It's the rule" or, "The director says so." Agency rules are the child care worker's own rules, and he enhances his authority when he answers a child's question about them. In the same vein, when a child questions a rule, it may be less to learn its rationale than to test the environment or to test the child care worker's consistency.

First, let us look at the structure of rules. No matter what *formal* rules the administration requires, they will be augmented by *informal rules* and *local rules.*

The ability to distinguish the sources of various rules will help the child care worker to implement them and to interpret them to the children in a way that is logical, consistent and satisfying. Rules can often be irritating to children, especially adolescents. The older youngster will frequently ask the why's and wherefore's of rules that seem to limit his freedom or prevent expression of age-appropriate behavior. Questions such as "Why can't I leave earlier?", "Why can't I return later?", "Why can't I do this or the other?", all have to do with activities restricted by rules.

Formal rules are made to meet administrative necessities and cannot be changed. Laws, liability insurance, personnel practices, for example, must be lived with and are easiest to explain. Children accept such rules because they are unequivocal, impersonal and readily understood. Staff has little conflict about following abstract rules.

Informal rules (they may be called consequential rules) are less rigid and lend themselves to interpretation and bending. For instance, all children must be in bed by 10 o'clock, but under certain conditions some may stay up later. Some will say, "Rules are made to be broken," but the question is, "How often?" and, of course "Under what circumstances?"

The next level in the hierarchy of rules is that of local or ground rules that come about by common agreement of staff and children. These rules can become confusing when instituted out of personal considerations or idiosyncracies. One child care worker may say one thing and another something else. Care must be taken that rules are clear and consistently applied. Two anecdotes illustrate how children can be confused by arbitrary changes in simple directions.

1) Smoking has long been banned at the dining room table because the table was burned due to carelessness. Staff who instituted the ban enforced it by themselves not smoking at the table. A substitute child care worker learns of the ban and says to the group, "I smoke at the table, so you, too, can smoke at the table."

2) Charles's chore for the week is to wash dishes. A child care worker teaches him how to do it. On another day, a second child care worker watches Charles doing the dishes and criticizes him: "That's not the way to wash dishes." Charles replies he was taught this method. The child care worker retorts, "When I'm on duty, you do it my way."

The Individual Versus the Group

Child care workers are under tremendous pressure in their daily work and often feel as if they have been put into a nutcracker when they try to negotiate the milieu. Pressures are felt not only from the demands of the children under their care, but from the clinic, school and, above all, administration. Most confusing for child care workers is the need to individualize their approach to the children and yet maintain the integrity of the group.

"Let Pete sleep late because . . ."
"Excuse Sam from breakfast because . . ."
"Don't push Jane to make her bed because . . ."
"Let Dave watch TV after lights out because . . ."

Child care workers know if they let one do it, all the rest want some deviation from the structure for themselves. The child care workers recognize that if everyone in the group is permitted to "do his own thing," group cohesion is destroyed, thereby spelling trouble for everyone, staff and children alike.

Yes, individual needs are important and must be met. However, the child care worker cannot permit individualization to such an extent that the group will be confused about rules, procedures and authority. Rules cannot be diluted to such extent that they become meaningless. They must be applied consistently and fairly, or chaos will result. Rules show that adults care, and even though children verbalize resentment, they will appreciate a fair and consistent application of them. And yet, a residential treatment setting is not a rigid organization, like the army, with a strictly controlled uniformity. The setting must allow for an individual approach within a structure designed for the program. How this is done requires a delicate balance of choices between the needs of the individual child and the group. Otherwise, a child care worker who gives a child special treatment will be accused of playing favorites, of having a "pet."

There are principles that help the child care worker walk the thin line between individual needs and the group, and that are useful in establishing a general therapeutic approach to children. It has been observed through experience that the group is acutely aware of the needs, both emotional and physical, of the individual children within it. Also, an intact group realistically perceives special needs of children at any given time. An obvious example is that of a youngster who has been ill, has just returned from the hospital, and requires a period of recuperation. The children will not resent the child care worker's extra attention to the patient, even though they themselves may be short-changed. In fact, the group will be observing the child care worker's behavior and probably evaluate the manner in which he is treating the child. The children will feel secure if the child care worker gives the patient adequate attention. The child care worker's reaction to the situation will indicate what can be expected if they are in a similar plight.

The rule of thumb is that the children will see any individual treatment as legitimate or illegitimate and, if it is not legitimate, will let the child care worker know by saying so directly or acting out. Staff also must know if the special treatment to be given is legitimate or not. Otherwise, the youngster may use the relationship to manipulate and, as a consequence, effect a breakdown of the structure.

For example, Jane was a very needy girl and all the child care workers responded to her demands for attention. Although needy themselves, the individuals in the group allowed Jane to get more individual attention than they did for a long time. But there came a point when the group felt she had outgrown the need for special attention and began complaining to staff about her. Through this process, Jane recognized that she no longer required the individual attention and gave up demanding it.

This vignette illustrates how the individuals in the group perceived Jane's growth before the staff became aware of it. The child care workers had to be sensitive to the group's message, which said, in effect, "It *was* legitimate to give Jane the special attention, but it no longer is."

Individualization has another meaning. Every child arrives at the residential treatment center with his own set of peculiarities, his symptoms, if you will. Some will be innocuous. Others can be annoying to staff and the other children. The child care worker must understand that the child did not select the symptoms and did not choose to be the way he is. His symptoms are defenses against his perception of the world as hostile; they are not of his making and may well not be under his control. To maintain a therapeutic attitude toward the child, the child care worker must accept and tolerate the presenting symptomatology. The youngster will eventually give up his symptoms when he feels safe enough to express his bottled up anger without fear of retaliation by the adults who are taking care of him.

It follows, then, that the child care worker must rethink his own prejudices about mental illness and any preconceived notions about the prospects for change. The child's lifelong experience has made him feel different from other children and, as a consequence, pessimistic about any positive outcome. To counteract the child's view of a bleak future for himself, the child care worker should always be optimistic, reassuring the child that it will not always be the way it is now.

Still another aspect of appropriate and necessary individualization is timing in response to periods of anxiety and crisis. The child care worker should allow sufficient time and space for a child to work through upsetting feelings before he reacts or attempts to intervene. Each child will need a different kind of response, based upon the child care worker's knowledge of the youngster.

Upon learning of some apparent misdeed, either from other children or staff, the child care worker ought not jump to conclusions. Delaying judgment will allow the child care worker to hear impartially the youngster's side of the story, permit enough time to listen calmly and attentively. Empathizing with the child's story will go a long way toward gaining his trust, and aid in correcting any distortions he may have regarding the fairness of adults.

Child care workers must be sensitive to the feelings stirred up in themselves in their work with children. Almost daily, they must review their own behavior toward children and ask themselves the question: "Am I doing this for myself, my own interest and needs, or am I doing it for the child?"

Group Meetings

Perhaps the most important tool the child care worker has at his disposal for creating cohesion in the living situation is the group meeting. It provides an opportunity to legitimate expressions of discontent among the members of the group as well as toward staff members. It is the best opportunity for planning. It gives the child care workers a vantage point from which to observe the interactions among the youngsters in the group. An additional value lies in bringing together all of the youngsters for a positive learning experience in group interaction.

The children in the group should be able to use the opportunity to express, without fear of retaliation, their feelings and opinions about the environment they live in. For the child care worker to produce a therapeutic atmosphere permitting freedom of expression by the children, he must feel secure about himself and be able to take criticism without being defensive. At the same time, the group meeting cannot become a free-for-all, an overly permissive forum. Limits must be set, as in all other group activities.

To hold successful group meetings, the child care worker must keep in mind three conditions: 1) *place and time*, 2) *ground rules*, 3) *agenda.*

1) The child care worker must first decide where and when he will conduct the group meeting. The decision is of utmost importance and should take into consideration convenience and comfort for all members. Some child care workers prefer to hold meetings in the evening after dinner, others shortly after snack time. In any event, if the child care worker has decided to plan a weekly meeting (a suitable frequency), it is desirable to hold it at the same time and place each week. Consistency reinforces the overall structure of the program.

2). The ground rules should be uncomplicated and understood by the group from the outset. Simple rules, such as one child speaking at a time, no yelling, everyone remaining in his seat during the meeting, and the like, are conducive to an orderly discussion of issues by the group. After the first few meetings, the group will recognize the format, and repeating the rules won't be necessary. Experience shows that as the child care worker becomes relaxed and confident of the outcome, the group will, in turn, be less anxious and more productive.

3) The formal agenda can be written or conveyed verbally to the group at the beginning of the meeting. As the leader, the child care worker determines when the meeting should end, allowing sufficient time for all the business to be conducted, yet not enough time for boredom to intrude and lead to disorganization. Consequently, the length of the meeting is determined by the age and kinds of children the child care worker has under his care.

A typical agenda should organize the content into concrete items (such as chores), gripes, and planning. Frequently, the child care worker has to intervene to help in the decision-making process. The productiveness of the group meeting is in the decisions arrived at by the members. For its outcome to have meaning for the children, the meeting must conclude with a sense of accomplishment, an indication of the resolution of some of the problems mentioned and something to look or work for in the immediate future.

The time allowed for gripes should be limited, but enough for full expression and discussion. Complaints about other children or staff should have a full hearing, but should be limited only to those attending the meeting. Gripes about staff present at the meeting should be handled maturely and not defensively. Probably the most difficult part of the meeting for child care workers is listening to children's complaints about themselves. It offers the worker, however, an opportunity to explain why he did such and such, or to reveal his human side by admitting error and apologizing if this is appropriate.

Planning for activities — outings, games, picnics, and so on — can be the pleasurable part of the meeting. The child care worker can also use planning to his advantage. The staff work schedule usually calls for 2 days off duty in sequence. One way of bridging the absence is for the child care worker to plan activities to take place when he is away.

Youngsters will be thinking of him during his absence, and on his return, he can start his tour of duty by referring to or implementing plans made earlier.

Sensitive Issues in Child Care

Adolescence

Under the most benign conditions, living with adolescent boys and girls is difficult. Too old to be treated like a child, not old enough to be given the prerogatives of an adult, the adolescent in our society is neither fish nor fowl. And if life is troublesome for the adolescent at home and in the community, it is doubly hard for him or her in placement.

The child care worker working with adolescents must have some awareness of normal adolescent behavior before he goes overboard and classifies commonly expected behavior as pathological.

Three main points ought to be borne in mind: 1) ambivalence in the adolescent, 2) ambivalence in the adult, and 3) the value of conflict and rebellion.

Ambivalence in the Adolescent. The younger adolescent wants the privileges of both childhood and adulthood and views the responsibility of the latter as an onerous burden. He sees no connection between increased adult privilege and increased responsibility.

In contrast, the older adolescent can see better the corresponding relationship between privilege and responsibility. His critical concern is a fear of failure in carrying out the responsibility involved. Also, he fears the liberation and indulgence of the new forces and impulses inside himself. He cannot be certain that he can control them once they are free.

Child care workers will encounter problems in assigning responsibility to the younger and the older adolescent and should have insight into the sources of the difficulties. Along with recognizing the physical fatigue (often considered laziness) accompanying pubescence, the child care worker should realize that the adolescent experiences psychological difficulties in the assignment of chores and the expectation of performing them well.

The young adolescent still desires privileges connected with childhood, as well as those related to adolescence. He is torn between the struggle for independence and the comfort and safety of childhood dependence. On this basis, the youngster would naturally tend to view assignment of chores as restrictive, burdensome and, possibly, threatening to former childish relationships with adults, particularly parental surrogates, such as child care workers represent. In working with the younger adolescent, it is most fruitful to assign chores carefully and with discrimination. Overloading the youngster with new responsibilities might only increase his ambivalence and his struggle with the child care worker. Even though the younger adolescent may seem chronologically and physically ready, the assignment of chores should be kept to a healthy minimum.

Adults should explain the purpose of chores as sharing in community living and privileges. They must exercise patience and provide some help in doing the work. This might make the assumption of more responsibility less painful and more valuable. Mutual understanding and good communication are of utmost importance for the young adolescent and the significant adults who are responsible for his care.

In working with older adolescents, it is often illuminating to child care workers to learn that they fear failure or loss of control in assuming concomitant privileges and responsibilities. Too often, child care workers see only the external bravado put forth by the adolescents in their many demands for increased privileges and responsibility. Child care workers tend to become involved with pointing out the relationship between these two things, and underestimate the deeper need for their help and support. It is critical that the child care worker communicate his trust in the youngster's ability to handle privilege and responsibility. Even if the youngster "goofs" somewhat at first, it is important that the adult accept his motivation to succeed, rather than rescind a privilege too promptly. Firm, well explained limits on inappropriate demands will give the youngster a sense of relief, for he really knows he can't handle some of what he asks for. Such an approach will strengthen his trust in adults and allow him to rely on their judgment when he needs to. Praise should be forthcoming when he assumes and handles privileges and responsibility well, rather than an attitude of mere acceptance of unexpected compliance. Praise reinforces the desire to do well and allays some of the anxiety about failing. Again, a vital relationship of mutual understanding, trust and good communication can be strengthened.

In a residential treatment setting where both levels of adolescents are in care and treatment, opportunities must be created for granting privileges and concomitant responsibility. For example, day trips may be allowed with appropriate limits on how time is spent and the time expected for return. Dating privileges can be utilized in a healthy way. Parties can be planned with the adolescents assuming leadership and responsibility for them.

Ambivalence in the adults. Child care workers may be overly aware of the youngsters' weaknesses and overemphasize the pathology described in social history and, perhaps, exhibited in placement. They may feel threatened by a reawakening of their own past fears, conflicts and yearnings, their own doubts about themselves and frustrations. There may be some jealousy over the opportunities of youth that may seem to be disappearing for them.

Any of these bases for ambivalence (and it is important for the child care worker to raise any other sources to conscious awareness) can lead to overprotection of the adolescent or excessive efforts to free the adolescent prematurely.

Value of conflict and rebellion. Some child care workers see all adolescent rebellion as irritating and inevitable, and rather superficially as "growing pains." There is a productive aspect to rebellion that allows for testing self-assertiveness. The adolescent needs to be provided with something constructive and tangible to fight. Otherwise, he cannot carve out a sound value system. In this light, rebellion has the potential for development of increased and needed self-assertion, leadership qualities and creativity for the adolescent emerging into adulthood.

In working with adolescents, this has important implications. Besides providing tangible limits for their own security, the child care worker must give them something worthwhile to question, criticize and disagree with. The child care worker should be prepared to yield on less crucial issues after allowing the youngsters to plead for and convince him of their case. To be too permissive or too authoritarian, without room for question and discussion, can confuse and inhibit the youngsters' development of leadership strengths, value systems and creative thinking.

Child care workers have to have confidence in their capacity, skill and wholeness, as human beings and adults, to be able to tolerate rebellion in adolescents and to guide this particular stage of development constructively.

Anger and Violence

The child care worker is in a position of great power, and frequently the imposition of his will through a request or demand can arouse angry responses. Sometimes the angry reactions are greatly exaggerated and out of proportion to the request. The irrational anger is manifested in different ways — silent resistance, a barrage of profanity, or at the extreme, physical violence. An action-reaction system of this kind can be described as follows: Counselor's authority → child's negative transference → irrational anger.

This representation is meant to show that a countervailing negative transference is provoked in the child when the child care worker assumes the role of a parental figure. The youngster then reacts as he did in unpleasant experiences with his parents, whom he does not trust. Also, a part of the anger exhibited is caused by the overdependent position in which the child finds himself, triggering the essential struggle of the adolescent between wanting to be independent and yet still needing the security of adults caring for him.

All too often, anger is generated in a child care worker when a youngster defies his authority, especially when this is done in front of a group. The child care worker's anger manifests itself in many ways (resistiveness, opposition, even threats) and if an appropriate safety valve is not available to channel the anger, the offending child may become the target of physical attack.

Physical attack on a staff member by a child, or by a staff member on a child, is a serious matter that must be handled administratively. A policy and procedure must exist to handle any act of violence on the part of a child or staff member. The administrator on duty must determine whether the violence is likely to continue and must prevent its recurrence. Further assessment must also determine 1) the likelihood of its continuing recurrence over a longer period of time, and 2) the institution's capacity for

35

effectively preventing and controlling such incidents. Against the background of those judgments, it must then be finally determined whether the offender — child or staff member — is to be discharged.

The development of sound attitudes and the capacity for healthy interpersonal relationships in children are significantly hindered by the use of force by the staff to impose one's will on another person. Consequently, it can readily be seen that violence by children or staff (except force used to restrain a child from doing injury to himself or someone else) is in clear and direct violation of the basic philosophy and practice of Linden Hill's program.

The child care worker has to learn to handle his own feelings in a manner that will result in an attitude toward the child that is therapeutically helpful. Anger can be provoked in a child by antitherapeutic handling. Thoughtless comments, nagging, wild statements, useless interpretations, smothering favoritism, challenging expectations beyond a child's readiness to perform, inconsistency, harsh words or orders — all can arouse a child's anger. Antitherapeutic attitudes can play havoc in a group situation, causing great turmoil. Most situations where youngsters are upset can be traced directly either to poor handling of the children or to staff dysfunction leading to an untherapeutic climate in the building.

It is obvious, then, that child care workers must continually be aware of their own feelings and how they are expressed and directed if the workers are to have a beneficial effect on the children under their care.

Stealing

Several types of stealing can be identified and dealt with appropriately.

1) It is ***compulsive stealing*** when a child takes things from other children out of envy or to satisfy some need.

2) *Mischievous stealing,* which involves taking property belonging to the institution, is regarded as antisocial behavior.

3) *Malicious stealing* is often deliberately planned to get someone else into trouble or to upset another child.

Compulsive stealing stems from severe behavior problems. Punishment alone will intensify the problem. A child care worker should be careful to convey a desire to help the child with the stealing problem. It is necessary to point out that the child can receive this help only from his therapist.

Mischievous stealing often involves more than one child and is usually connected with boredom or hostility against the residence. The children can be dealt with directly by the child care workers, provided no serious damage has been done. In the case of serious damage, the situation should be called to the attention of the administrative staff. Group pressure can be used effectively in these instances. At times it is necessary to hold the entire group responsible, to help them face the reality that group members are partly responsible if they have knowledge of such activity and do nothing to correct it. Classrooms and offices are particularly vulnerable spots, and care must be exercised to see that these areas are properly locked and that windows are closed. A well structured program of interesting activities can help to minimize this kind of stealing.

Malicious stealing is differentiated from compulsive stealing because it is done deliberately to hurt someone, as, for example, when a child takes something from one child and puts it in another child's room. Another example is the theft of an article that has particular meaning to the owner. This type of stealing must be dealt with by the child care worker directly. The use of group pressure is of questionable value.

When a child tells the child care worker that something of his is missing, the child care worker should get a description of the article and help the child explore the possibility of its being mislaid or loaned before jumping to the conclusion it was stolen. Once these possibilities are eliminated, the child care worker should never assume full responsibility for locating the missing article. The child often tries to get the child care worker to say that he will definitely do something about finding or replacing the article. It is necessary to point out the responsibility the child has in helping to discover the whereabouts of the article.

Carelessness, being too free to lend, borrowing without direct permission, can lead to the loss of articles and the assumption that they have been stolen. The staff should point out to the child that careless handling of his belongings produces situations where stealing is more likely to occur. This is the way the child can be helped to minimize the stealing problem.

The child whose money is stolen is often as responsible as the child who takes it. Children can invite stealing by flaunting their possessions in front of others and sharing with only a select few. Pointing this out affords an opportunity to help an individual child to see the effects of his behavior on others. This does not mean that a child has to share to prevent stealing, but that he should learn to avoid deliberately creating envy in others.

There will be times when it is necessary to search rooms to find the stolen article. The room search is something that should be done as seldom as possible and only after consultation with the child care worker and evaluation of the effects on the group as a whole. When rooms are searched, it should be done with the knowledge of the children, and every room should be gone over. The impression should not be created that some children are trusted and not others. However, if the child care worker is pretty certain that a particular child took the article and therefore feels that only the one room should be searched, it is best to tell only the child whose room is searched.

Stealing outside the residence (shoplifting) is also handled in a particular fashion. When the child care worker learns that items have been stolen by a child or a group of children from a store or other place of business, he must take immediate action. The items taken must be collected, if possible, and the child or the group interviewed to obtain the details. The message conveyed to the youngsters by the child care worker is that he is disappointed because his trust has been abused. He gave them the privilege of leaving the residence because of his confidence that their behavior would be exemplary.

It must be made clear that the stolen objects do not belong to the youngsters, but remain the property of the owner. The children have a choice of two alternatives: return the merchandise if it is not damaged, or pay for the merchandise and keep it. In making either choice, the children must negotiate with the shopkeeper or owner of the items in the presence of the child care worker. By handling the shoplifting episode in this manner, the child care worker helps the child to face the consequences of his behavior.

Sex

The range of sexual behavior that may become evident among some of the children in the child care setting includes sexual language and gestures, individual and group masturbation, exhibitionism, and attempts to promote sexual experience. These manifestations may appear in (groups of) children of the same sex (often mislabeled "homosexual" behavior), as well as in mixed groups. It should be noted that provocation leading to the expression of sexual feelings may be induced by internal stimuli or, as is often the case, by peer association. In addition, acting-out behavior may be due to adult-child stimulation.

A feature that has been observed in children is an escalating quality in sexual behavior. Starting with the unchecked use of erotically charged language and gestures, the behavior may move rapidly in stages to overt sexual acting out.

The language of swearing is usually of an erotic nature and can be categorized under several broad headings. 1) Sexual language is the most general vehicle for expression of anger; bursts of rage on the part of the child are accompanied by profanity or sexual reference. 2) Cursing is used to overcome fear or frustration due to helplessness. 3) "Bad" words are used to be "naughty," to "shock" the adult, as a sign of growing up, or to titillate. 4) Certain words are spoken out of habit because of a limited vocabulary.

Types of Question

Questions about sex that children ask may fall within the following categories:

1) *Out of curiosity.* Some of the questions and sex play may be of an infantile nature, which in a younger child may result in "playing doctor." An early interest in sex is a natural part of the slow process of growing up. Some adolescents are just beginning to feel safe enough to experiment.

2) *For information.* The adolescent's acute awareness of his sexuality, bound up with the poor relationship he has with his parents, has left him with information or misinformation from outsiders, and his own active imagination. Wonderment and distortions may trouble a youngster and he easily becomes worried about his sexuality and easily imagines he is "different" or abnormal.

3) *Because of anxiety.* Some children are anxious over the frequency of masturbation or about sexual acts they have committed, while others are extremely concerned over their poor relationships with the opposite sex.

4) *As a means of provoking staff.* Some children have an acute sense for finding a "soft spot" that can be used to trigger a reaction from a child care worker. Certain sex questions or behavior are found that stimulate a child care worker to reveal himself, to the detriment of the group. A child care worker should be on the lookout for indirect questions.

A seemingly innocuous type of sexual acting out that straddles all of the foregoing categories takes the form of inquiries aimed at getting information about the sex life of a staff member. Sexual conversations often focus on fantasies about adult sexual behavior and sometimes these contain thinly veiled anxiety and curiosity about parents, rather than adults in general.

A child care worker should be alert to the motives of the child who asks the question. For example, he should not leap to the conclusion that such a question as "How's your sex life?" is necessarily an attack on him. Neither should he think that childish ignorance is the usual source of an inquiry; more than once child care workers have been duped by the seeming interest of one or two children who want to talk about sex in the guise of obtaining information. A child care worker who does not know the children and is insensitive to their needs may find himself the supplier of a vicarious source of sexual excitement.

Controlling Language

Sexual language should not be reacted to with shock or surprise, but it should not be accepted by any staff member. Since such language is socially unacceptable, the child care worker attempts to help the youngster to substitute some more acceptable form of expression. Calling attention to the child's self-respect, as well as respect for others, is in order. The logic of this kind of social control is that public sexual language, or behavior, for that matter, infringes on the freedom of others, is socially disapproved, and produces emotional difficulties in other children. Thus, although the fact of sexuality is not disapproved, it is classified as a private activity. Youngsters are able to understand the logic of firm but clearly defined social control of sex.

Perhaps the *single greatest error* made by the adults dealing with troubled youngsters is in underestimating the amount of guilt that is generated by sexual thoughts and activity.

Child care workers should supply sexual information to children whenever it is requested and the request is considered credible. The child care worker should evaluate the child and at the same time be aware of feelings within himself that are generated by the question.

Although child care workers come from a variety of

backgrounds and age groups, and therefore bring with them different emotional investments and knowledge, they ought to be able to deal with sex in a calm, unemotional and intelligent way.

Runaways

Deviant behavior in the children manifests itself in different ways. One is running away from the institution. This is disconcerting not only to the staff, but to the group. Even though the children may seem to be unaffected, they are perturbed about it on some level.

It is usual for one or two other children to be aware beforehand of the runaway's intention. They may have learned because he told them what he was planning to do and, perhaps, asked for money, instructions, diversion of staff, a dummy in bed to fool the child care worker, and so forth. If the child did not tell other children directly, some or all may have sensed it through his behavior.

If the child care worker can make the important distinction between a *planned* runaway and an *impulsive* runaway, he will be able to handle the situation in the best therapeutic manner. The difference is quite discernible, and from the type of runaway, the mode of action and reaction will flow for the child care worker.

Children run away as a result of stimuli from without or stimuli from within. The former may be the less difficult problem to handle from a management point of view. The youngster may be making an adjustment to placement but something in the environment triggers his action. He may not want to leave the institution, but he sees the milieu as forcing him to leave for his safety — his feeling of being cared for is threatened and an overwhelming sense of self-defense and self-protection takes over and motivates him to leave the institution. After weighing everything, he chooses the lesser of two evils, concluding that he will be safer away from the institution than in it. Perhaps the child care worker is not providing the protection the child needs. Only a careful review of the incident will reveal if the child care worker was responsible. The child care worker should look for **scapegoating.** Was the child especially picked on by his peers? If so, was his anger toward the bullies appropriate or did he feel defenseless? A child who cannot fight back or retaliate is likely to abscond as a way of avoiding the situation. If he has a home to go to, he will probably run to parents or a relative, but it is also common for such a youngster to roam the streets and hide somewhere, feeling sorry for himself and yearning for someone to take care of him.

Another closely related reason is clinically called **homosexual panic.** This can be a reaction of either a boy or girl to a sexually stimulating environment. It is a most devastating situation for a child to be in fear of actual or threatened sexual abuse by more powerful peers. In his mind, the only course of action is to run away, to escape his real or imagined exploiters. Also, an attraction to homosexual play will coincide with fantasies of participation and enjoyment, and will be defended against psychologically by running away. In any case, the child is vulnerable, fearful, alone, abandoned.

The main indication of the runaway caused by internal stimuli is **depression.** For the child, depression is equated with being lifeless. To overcome this passivity, the child surges into activity as a defense against death. The runaway chooses a physical activity (doing something, anything) to relieve the anguish and suffering. Unfortunately for the child, running away may not relieve the pangs of suffering, and he or she may move on to an activity even more exciting by meeting and joining others in increasingly stimulating and self-destructive behavior.

The youngster's anger at his parents for placing him away from home often causes him to have fantasies about killing them for their rejection. These fantasies are converted into fears that the parents may actually be dead. The child seeks affirmation that his thoughts did not kill, so he runs home to make certain that they are alive. Another variation on this theme is exhibited by the child of divorced parents who blames himself for his parents' separation. He hopes he can be instrumental in effecting a reunion and creating a home of peace, tranquility and love.

What does the child care worker do first? He must make some assessment of the conditions that caused the child to leave. If he believes that the child left because of external stimuli, he should try to learn from others in the group exactly what happened. Sensitive handling and reliance on his relationship with the children will usually provide some answers. The concern of the child care worker not only will strengthen his relationship with the group, but may evoke a similar concern in the other children. Also, each member of the group wants to feel protected by an adult, regardless of protestation to the contrary; whatever the child care worker does and says to individuals and the group will convey to them what he probably would do were any of them the victim.

At whatever stage the child care worker is involved in the youngster's return, reassurance and protection should be the message the child receives — certainly not fear of discipline. He should be helped to cope with subsequent incidents either by himself, with his own resources, or by relying on the child care worker's authority to act on his behalf. In the case of a depressive reaction, the child care worker must act protectively to prevent the youngster from hurting himself. The child care worker should be sympathetic, but firm. The youngster should, in some cases, be restricted by curtailment of some sort of freedom. Depression can be treated only if anxiety exists, that is, if the urge to be self-destructive becomes ego-dystonic, meaning "I don't enjoy doing it." Listening to the child express feelings is often helpful.

Anxiety brought on by separation from home and family should be handled a bit differently. The child care worker should be sympathetic, also firm, but less involved in talking and listening than in cases of depression. Letter writing and telephone calls to parents should be encouraged as a way of coping.

To repeat, the watchword is to avoid generalization about causes. All runaways do not stem from the same origins. Careful analysis will help develop a sensible approach to each.

Death and the Mourning Process

At some time in their career, child care workers will be involved in the death of someone close to a child or to all the children under their care. It may be the parent of one of the children, a staff member, or one of the children. In such situations, the impact on the child varies according to the age of the youngster, as well as the closeness and age of the deceased. The death of a parent will usually have the greatest impact. The impact of the death of a staff member will depend on how significant he was to the children. The depth of grief over the death of one of the children will depend on the child's relationship with the other children.

In any event, any death produces strong feelings of sadness, bewilderment, anger and guilt, and these feelings pass through stages. For the child care worker to be helpful, he must remember that the child should experience a working through of his grief. Simply stated, the stages of mourning are: announcement, acknowledgment, mourning, renewal.

The child care worker will become involved with the child at various stages of his grief, and he has to know how far the child has progressed in the mourning process in order to do and say what is appropriate and to feel that he is doing what is right.

If the child care worker received notification of the death of a child's parent or relative and has the responsibility to tell the child, several decisions have to be made, among them, the choice of the appropriate time and place to talk. It must also be decided if another staff member is to be present.

The child does not have to be told immediately; a suitable time may be selected. If the call comes during the night and the child is asleep, the announcement can wait until morning. The news and the child's reaction to it are very personal, and a quiet place away from the group is preferable. Chairs should be placed so as to provide a feeling of closeness. Announcement to the child should be made calmly and sympathetically, with the knowledge that there is really no "right" way of conveying tragic news. The reaction to the news will be different with each child and, again, depends on the relationship. The child care worker or some other staff member with whom the child is close can help the child to accept the irrevocability of the loss. Appropriate questions about the deceased are in order, to help the child begin to experience the sense of loss.

The mourning process will start with the expression of feelings stimulated by the loss. The child care worker should encourage crying as a legitimate show of feeling. He must not convey to the child that crying is a sign of weakness and that he should hold back tears. Unfortunately, our society frowns on crying, and too often it is looked upon as appropriate only for babies. Accordingly, statements such as "Be brave," or "Hold your chin up," should be avoided. It is better to remain quiet and supportive than to say anything that will interfere with the mourning process. On no account should one make statements that depreciate or deny the awful reality of loss. Such denials constitute a refusal to share the child's grief.

Sometimes it may seem that the child's expression of grief is exaggerated in light of his relationship to the deceased. The child care worker should remember that previous losses may be connected and mourned with this one.

The fourth stage, getting on with the business of living, takes place afterward. The length of time this takes again depends on the child and the situation. Encouragement in resuming activities that were dropped and returning to regular routines are important at this time. Taking part in the funeral rites is also important in the mourning process. Wherever possible, the child should attend the funeral with the family and participate with them in their grief.

In the event of the death of a staff member, the mourning and working through of grief is the same, except that it becomes a group process. The announcement should take place in an assembly of children and staff. It is important that as many staff and children as possible hear the news and experience the shock together. Again, time and place are selected to give optimum opportunity for the fact to be learned and absorbed. Afterward, the children may return to their living quarters with their child care workers, who can continue the working through in smaller groups. If it happens that the children and staff cannot all attend the funeral services, a memorial service should be held at the institution, with the children and staff participating.

The death of a child should be handled in the same manner as that of a staff member.

The experienced reader will probably recall that identical stages of the mourning process take place when a significant member of the staff leaves the institution. The staff members' departure likewise evokes strong feelings of loss and anger. The child care worker handles these feelings in the manner we have described earlier. Wanting to alleviate some of his own guilt feelings about leaving, the staff member, however, may make unrealistic promises to the children, such as "I'll write," "I'll call," "I'll come to visit," "You can visit." Children remember these promises and in time the worker's failure to follow through reactivates the anger. It is unnecessary for the staff member to volunteer maintaining contact. If a child asks "Will you write?", the reply can be a simple "I'll try."

The Family

Mail and Letter Writing

Should the question ever arise whether children are restricted as to the number of letters they may write and receive and with whom they may correspond? Generally, it is understood that neither letter writing nor receiving is considered a privilege. Unless there is evidence, not mere suspicion, that personal mail may contain dangerous contraband, children should receive mail addressed to them. It can be an important connection with the "outside world" and meaningful relatives and friends.

The child care worker should make certain that mail is given to the children each day that postal deliveries are made. A time and place should be set for the receipt of mail, but the less obvious the better. Child care workers should avoid congregating children army style and calling out the last name of the recipient. Imagine the feelings of the youngster who did not receive the mail he was expecting.

It is better to leave mail on a table for youngsters to take their own, or take the time to put a child's mail in his room, perhaps on the bed where he can see it. When a child asks whether he has mail, it means that he is expecting some, and the child care worker should show sensitivity to his disappointment by saying, "No, Joe, I'm sorry there wasn't any; perhaps tomorrow."

For some children, writing letters to friends and relatives is an activity used to maintain contacts prior to placement and to retain communication with parents. These youngsters find letter writing easy, and it often borders on a hobby. For others, writing is much more difficult. The question arises whether the child care worker should encourage children to write letters. Some children avoid writing letters to parents as a way of rejecting them. When this occurs, the child care worker is sometimes put in the position of carrying a message for the parents when they ask his intervention. "Why doesn't Jane write me?", "Can you get Bill to write to me?" are frequent demands made by mothers and, to a lesser degree, fathers. What should be the child care worker's reply to this sort of inquiry? He can reassure the parents that their child is all right and that their son or daughter will write them when he or she is ready to, perhaps soon.

The Child Care Worker and the Parent

Different child caring agencies relate to parents differently. In some instances, the placement agency not only welcomes the parents but encourages them to participate in the program, serving as volunteers in activity programs, on the board or in other ways. Involvement of the parents depends a great deal on not only their willingness but their ability to participate productively in the program.

When the parents are not capable of a positive involvement in the program, interaction between them and the child care workers is unclear. Parents have needs that have to be satisfied, together with those of their children in placement, if there is to be a cooperative effort to realize the benefits of placement and treatment, rather than parental interference in the treatment plan. (For example, what happens at home on a visit can influence the child profoundly.)

Admission to placement causes the eruption of many different feelings in the child, siblings, parents and close relatives. The child may be placed despite parents' open or covert opposition. The parents may act under pressure from school, neighbors, friends, professionals, or even the authorities. The family may disagree within itself on the necessity or wisdom of placement. Conflict may be increased by restrictions on visiting, the indefiniteness of diagnosis and prognosis, and the difficulty in understanding psychiatric terminology and treatment methods.

Parents react differently to placement. In some, we see the "dumped child syndrome": once the child is placed the parents lose interest and no longer make any attempt to maintain contact. On the other hand, sometimes one parent, usually the mother, is overambitious and obsessively anxious, believing that no one can understand or properly care for her child except herself. Such a mother suffers severe anxiety when separated from her child. She may complain about the poor care her child is receiving and threaten to withdraw the child from placement. This mother will also regard signs of independence that the child care worker and therapist consider improvement as the child's getting "worse." A common comment from such a mother, when confronted with self-assertive behavior, is, "He never used to do that."

In relating to such an anxious mother, the child care worker can help prevent the parent's sabotage of treatment by appropriate attention to the parent's needs. Recognition of the parent's emotional state is in order, rather than rebuffing her.

Family members are often divided in opinion regarding placement and what should be done to help the child. The more dominant spouse may have insisted on placement, while the other may consider care at home as the only solution. This situation is found particularly when parents are separated or divorced. The child care worker can easily get caught up in such struggles, just as the child has been, and must guard against antagonizing one parent by seeming to side with the other.

Intense guilt reactions may occur in parents who feel they are to blame for the child's condition. They feel impelled to do everything for the child, to respond to his every demand. Their guilt is often so extreme that it must be projected onto the staff or the institution. Shifting blame to the other parent, to teachers, or to some event is another form of projection.

Child care workers do best by not becoming embroiled in the projections and by helping to alleviate the guilt through reassurance. The child care worker often comes face to face with parental disharmony and parental guilt as they are manifested in recrimination by one parent against the other. Hostilities pent up through the years break forth when a mother or father, guilty concerning his or her deficiencies as a parent, ridicules the other for the failings that he or she thinks put the child in placement. The battle is noted by the child, who is often proficient in splitting the parents. In all probability, the child care worker has already observed the same techniques used by the child to split the staff. As each parent seeks to gain comfort from the staff, the child care worker must avoid showing favoritism toward one parent.

It is not unusual for child care workers to be uneasy in their contact with parents and as a consequence to inadvertently side with them. Child care workers must avoid being used by parents as message carriers or servants. By carefully and accurately assessing the relationship between child and parent, the child care worker can avoid being caught in the middle or used as a pawn in their individual love-hate, dependence-independence struggles.

Telephone contacts

Child care workers' communication with parents often takes place by telephone, and it is here that workers may find themselves trapped in sticky situations from which it is difficult to extricate themselves. Certain basic principles govern the use of the telephone. Children are encouraged to initiate telephone calls themselves. It is for this reason youngsters are given designated times to call their parents. This procedure allows the child to determine if he wants to make the call and speak with his parents, and gives the child care worker a handle to set limits for an overly anxious and dependent youngster who is having separation problems.

Child care workers must intervene protectively between parents and the child. The telephone is a remote, safe, almost impersonal, means for conveying hostility. When the phone is hung up, the interaction is abruptly completed — no eye-to-eye engagement, no tangible physical presence to cope with. With this in mind, child care workers should talk with the parents who are calling and try to elicit from them in a courteous and friendly way the purpose for the call and whether the parents can wait for the child to call them. This sort of intervention is especially important if the parent has bad news, such as death of a family member, hospitalization, accident, etc. It is much better for the child care worker to be involved in the handling of such situations from the beginning.

The following scenario illustrates the pitfalls of thoughtless handling:

Telephone rings.

Child Care Worker: Hello, Linden Hill.
Voice: Hello, this is Marty's mother. Can I
                   talk to him?
Child Care Worker: Hold on.

Child care worker hangs receiver on phone box and walks toward Marty's room. He finds Marty intently working on a model.

Child Care Worker:	Marty, your mother is on the phone and wants to talk to you.
Marty: (sullenly)	I'm busy, I don't want to talk to her.
Child Care Worker:	(argumentatively) What's the matter with you? Your mother is on the phone waiting for you.
Marty: (irritated)	I don't care, leave me alone. I'm doing something.
Child Care Worker:	Look, she's on the phone and it's costing her money. The least you can do is say "hello."
Marty: (angrily)	Leave me alone. (Breaks piece of model) See what you made me do, you bum.
Child Care Worker:	Don't talk to me like that, Marty, if you know what's good for you.

Marty curses. The child care worker shrugs his shoulders, leaves Marty's room and walks to the telephone.

Child Care Worker:	Mrs. Moore, I'm sorry but Marty doesn't want to talk to you.
Mrs. Moore:	What do you mean he doesn't want to talk to me? What's going on up there? What are you doing to my son? When he comes home, he acts worse than he did before he went up there, how come?
Child Care Worker:	I don't know.

Visiting Day

The question frequently arises regarding who should visit the child in placement. Some consider visiting day an opportunity for everyone to get together, a sort of family reunion with not only the parents, but brothers, sisters and other relatives. Although there are positives to such a "gathering of the clan," for some children in placement there are negatives that should be considered.

First, the child in placement may not really understand the reason he is not at home. Adults may have explained in one way or another that it is for his own good, or that his parents cannot take care of him properly, or that his behavior necessitated placement, etc., but often the child sees placement as punishment for something he cannot really comprehend. This is especially the case when brothers and sisters are still living at home, and even more so if the parents are together. The child in placement asks, "Why me?"

Second, the child who is visited longs to be with his parents and looks forward to the day when they visit him. When brothers and sisters accompany the parents, the effect of the visit is diluted because he must share the precious time with his parents. If the siblings are younger and become bored and restless, the parents' attention will be diverted to quiet or control the children.

The most disquieting period is when the family departs. Watching his parents leave exacerbates the child's feelings of abandonment. The child care workers receive the brunt of this anger after the visit.

When parents come to see their children on a designated visiting day, they are expected to adhere to a structure set for the visiting hours. This is especially necessary in situations where the parents, too, are disturbed. All parents arriving before visiting time should be asked to wait outside and reminded that they should avoid coming early in the future. If they intrude, the administrator on duty should be notified. If parents arrive much too early, they may be asked to leave the grounds and return at the proper time.

The regular chores of the children must be completed before they are permitted to be with their visitors. Parents should not be allowed to spend any time in the children's rooms. Visitors often criticize the child for the way he keeps his room, or make demands upon him that have negative results.

When parents remain at the residence with their child, they should not be permitted to use kitchen facilities or food. They should be discouraged from bringing food, since the child has already eaten. In addition, no facilities such as TV should be available for their use.

If the child's visitors are tardy in leaving after the visiting hour, the child care worker should consider taking the child aside and quietly reminding him that it is time for visitors to leave. In this approach, the child is given the responsibility for letting his visitors know that visiting hours are over. It follows, of course, that if the child cannot carry out the responsibility, the child care worker will have to speak for him.

Day-by-Day Routines

Observation Is Treatment

The children who come into placement usually have
been subject to a great deal of emotional and physical
neglect. The child care worker looms large in importance
as he assumes the role of the nurturing and caring person
in the child's life and becomes responsible for making up
in some small but significant way the deficits in the child's
past.

For an infant, the mother's capacity for observation
determines the quality of care the child will receive. If she
is effective, she will be attuned to the noises and gestures
the infant makes and respond sensitively to them. She will
be able to respond to subtle variations of crying, and
distinguish whether the infant is in pain, hungry or
uncomfortable. It is the inability to recognize the early
signals the infant transmits that causes much of the later
trouble.

As the child grows and talks, the kind of parental
observation changes with the child's development.
Clothing, grooming, personal hygiene, eating and physical
appearance become focal points of observation. With each

61

stage of development, the nature of parental observation changes. Yet, the parent's involvement is still perceived by the child as caring, even though resentment may be expressed.

The child care worker must be a "parental" observer of the children under his care. Looking at a youngster in the morning to note complexion, arrangement of clothing, color combinations, suitability to weather, is in order. At any sign of illness, the child should be referred to the nurse. With younger or disorganized boys and girls, the child care worker must check fly zipper, shoe laces, socks, hair and teeth, plus an array of other personal items. Checking each child and complimenting when appropriate will be perceived as caring and will engender a feeling of security in the group. Furthermore, the more a child has been neglected in the past, the more he will have a sense of well-being from the attention paid to him.

It is not only a concerned look that makes a child feel secure and cared for. "Therapeutic" touching adds another dimension to the child care worker's relationship. It may seem odd to the reader to be reminded to touch, or that there is such a thing as "therapeutic" touching. If the child care worker stops to reflect on the occasions he has touched a child, he will recall that in almost every instance, physical contact was initiated by the worker because he was emotionally moved to do so. Touching was associated with a stirring from within, a feeling of momentary closeness, a gesture of friendship, a show of concern. Since the therapeutic aspect of touching cannot be underestimated, the child care worker must, however, planfully touch each child, especially the unappealing youngster. One can surmise that the child care worker is not the first adult who is turned off by the child and, for this reason, he must double his efforts to make up for the deprivation the youngster has experienced.

The First
2 Hours
of the Day

How the day begins is vital to children. Tension in both the staff and youngsters develops during the rush to get everyone up, dressed and fed, and chores done.

It is difficult for children to understand staff's occasional early morning curtness, or scoldings and admonitions. The tensions that develop during the first 2 hours affect children and carry over to the classroom. A youngster acts out his tenseness by being irritable and uncooperative. His ability to learn is interfered with. The school should be notified if a child has had a particularly bad time in the morning. Alerting the teaching staff will help them to prepare for the youngster's arrival.

Efforts to start the day in an atmosphere of relaxation will provide the child with a sense of assurance and security. For example, child care workers should limit discussion to immediate issues. This is no time for arguments about activities that will take place in the afternoon.

Going
to
School

In addition to group living, child care workers and children are closely related to an important sector of the residential program — the academic school. Cooperation with teachers and the school program is begun by seeing to it that children are prepared for classes and arrive on time. If a child is unavoidably detained or absent because of a home visit, illness or any other reason, the principal at the school should be notified. If an excuse note is required, it should be supplied promptly.

In preparing children for school, the child care worker has to be watchful of every child in his group. He must know what the child should take along with him. One child is forgetful about his books, another about combing his hair, another about wearing clothing appropriate to the weather. Children who are neatly and comfortably dressed and properly groomed feel cared for.

Many children in residential treatment have histories of school failure, and therefore much trepidation about attending classes. The child care worker who gives encouragement and support helps to overcome feelings of anxiety and inadequacy. Consequently, a display of interest in what a child is doing in school will give the child care worker clues to sources of the child's anxiety and hints about where he needs support most.

Return from school requires as much of the child care worker's attention as the preparations for school. Child care workers must be at the residence in ample time to welcome children back. Some children will return from school having had a satisfying and productive day; others will in varying degrees have had an unproductive, even frustrating experience in school. Child care workers must observe each child and be sensitive to any outward display of affect that calls for their attention. The children who should change from school to play clothing should be reminded of this, if they have not already thought of it.

Snacks should be ready for the children by the time they return from school. Children should be helped to quiet down for the 10 or 15 minutes it takes to consume the food and drink. Encouragement by child care workers to participate calmly in snack time will prevent children from "grabbing and running."

The Last
2 Hours
of the Day

The last 2 hours of the day also deserve special attention. With the approach of bedtime, the program is geared toward a tapering off of activity and preparation of the children for a restful sleep. Any help given a child to ready himself for bedtime may well be more important than anything else done for him during the day. Study hour, undressing, showering, snacks, quiet talk, are all activities conducive to a tranquilizing atmosphere. If through purposeful effort we prepare children to enjoy 10 hours of unbroken sleep, we have gone a long way toward settling them down, making them less anxious, less tense and, in general, more comfortable.

When a child is in bed, short conversations with the child care workers are slowly replaced by more casual remarks. Nonverbal contacts (such as tucking in) may replace verbal communication for those who need or enjoy them. On the other hand, kissing or back rubbing or other direct physical contact is avoided, although some children may request it. Such contacts usually create erotic stimulation, and with it fresh anxieties, negating the purpose of relaxing the child before he falls asleep.

Many children tend to be most confiding about their thoughts and feelings during this period. Child care workers should keep to a minimum the time spent dealing with this expression of anxiety. However, one must be careful to show interest in the child and not leave him with a feeling of being brushed off. This is a good time for the child care worker to help the child accept the reality of time-place. We should convey the idea that now is the time for sleep — "tomorrow we can talk."

The child care worker must avoid being manipulated into giving attention over and beyond that necessary to help the child relax. The children often act like toddlers who keep calling their parents back with a variety of excuses. Recognition of the desire by the child to control the adult will help to discourage this kind of demand.

Mature judgment will determine the amount of attention each child will need.

"Lights out" means that all the children are in their own rooms preparing for sleep. Anything that prevents them from sleeping should be removed or corrected. Owners of radios will sometimes leave the set turned on very softly. A check should be made to be certain that radios are off. Children will sometimes hide the set under the blankets or put it in a place where it cannot be seen. If the child has not heeded a warning, the child care worker may remove the radio from the room. Similarly, children will try to use flashlights to continue reading. It goes without saying that candles, along with other means of illumination, are prohibited. A standing rule, which must be kept, is that children are never permitted to smoke in their rooms. Some children will try to smoke in the lavatory after lights out, but this must not be allowed.

Additional "don'ts" are visiting in rooms and sleeping together. Children are to stay in their own rooms and are not permitted to visit each other under any pretext after lights out.

It is good practice for child care workers who are on night call to make periodic checks until about midnight.

Clothing

Before a youngster is admitted to Linden Hill, a basic clothing list is sent to the family. It is expected that each child will arrive with the clothing stipulated on this list. Some children, of course, will not come directly from home or will not have a family to provide the clothing. Upon a child's admission, the child care worker makes an inventory of the clothing he has brought and notes the missing items that have to be supplied by the parents or the agency. It is necessary to examine each piece of clothing to eliminate torn, outgrown or otherwise useless garments. These items have to be replaced.

This is the time when items of clothing should be marked with the child's name. The child care worker is responsible for a continuing inventory and check of the child's clothing. Whenever items are worn out, they should be replaced. The child care worker should discuss the need for items with the business manager, who will suggest where the items should be bought and some guidelines as to costs. A purchase order will be issued and the child care worker will go with the child and make the purchase.

Shopping with the child care worker is a learning experience for the child. The child should be helped to budget his purchases and to select clothing within the budget. When a purchase is made, the new item is added to the child's clothing inventory.

1) An inventory of each child's clothing is made by the child care worker together with the child. This involves removal of the child's clothing from the dresser drawers and from the closet (dusting and cleaning the drawers and closets), examination of all clothing to determine the need for repair and replacement, and notations on the inventory sheet provided for each child.

2) The inventory is used as a basis for determining the child's needs and for planning the shopping trip. Staff judgment should be exercised in permitting the child to make his or her own selection and purchase, whenever possible. Depending on the child's age and competence, and the type of article to be purchased, the shopping may even be done without a staff member present, especially with older and more responsible children.

3) The inventory should be made with the child as casually as possible. Inventory taking should be spaced for children in the group throughout the entire month, and made at least once every 6 weeks for every child. Once a month is preferable.

4) Excessive clothing in a child's room should be weeded out and hung in the spare room, properly tagged for the child's future use, or sent home for safekeeping. Clothing should not be purchased until it has first been determined that the garments are not available at home.

5) Child care workers and children should plan to use after-school hours and Saturdays to replenish wardrobes. Shopping trips are usually supervised by child care workers, although more mature children, shopping in

two's and three's, may be unsupervised when simple purchases are to be made. There should be a regular plan for every child, to avoid the need for last-minute heavy shopping trips.

6) No child should be permitted to build up an extravagant wardrobe by buying excessively beyond inventory.

Food

Mealtimes are sometimes filled with tension and expressions of dissatisfaction. Child care workers are all too familiar with the feelings of deprivation that are sparked at mealtimes. The anxiety children feel because of being away from home is often expressed by criticizing, in unmistakable language, the food that is set before them. All of their disappointment and feelings of being abandoned seem to be heightened at these times. It is no easy task for the child care worker to allay this anxiety.

We all know the emotional investment people put into eating. Children attach a great deal of feeling and significance to food. In their eyes, institutional food is seldom as good as home cooking, even though the child care worker prepares something special. The child care worker is confronted with the children's own feelings of rejection and deprivation when they compare the food at the residence with meals they get at home. They express anger at being placed away from home by attacking the quality of the food. If the food is not up to par, the child care worker can help to minimize the reaction by acknowledging the children's feelings and the difference in the food, and, at the same time, by trying to understand the message the youngsters are sending. Attempting to "sell" the food as just as good as food at home is generally of little value and leads to a dead end.

But the children must eat, and child care workers are expected to make mealtime as pleasurable as possible, knowing that while a child is complaining about the food, he is also observing the way it is served, how the table is arranged, and other things that set the tone of the meal.

The three key aspects of mealtime are: *the food itself; how it is prepared; how it is served.* Child care workers are involved all the way. If the food is prepared in a central kitchen, they may feel that they have no part in deciding menus, the choice of food and the way it is cooked, sizes of portions, etc. But such is not the case. Clearly, the child care workers must let the dietitian or cook know the children's reaction to the food, whether it is received with or without enthusiasm. If the meals are good, the child care worker should let it be known. Any information the child care worker can provide is in order. But children, especially adolescents, will favor certain foods that do not necessarily constitute a balanced diet. Food is the basis of nutrition and nutrition is the basis of good health. Consequently, child care workers must support sound nutrition policies.

Child care workers must evaluate the food on the basis of the children's taste, and not their own. Some child care workers like spicy food, while others are sensitive to any piquant food. Preferences should not be imposed on the children, nor should negative comments be made in front of them. Children have to be helped to separate their feelings about the food served from feelings of homesickness.

Esthetic considerations are certainly a component in the serving of food. The table should be set with some thought to providing pleasing color and design. China should be of a uniform pattern, as should knives, forks and spoons. Necessary condiments should be placed conveniently in the center of the table. Family style is the preferred way of serving food. Appropriate serving forks and spoons are to be used. Except for cookouts and picnics, paper plates and plastic flatware are to be avoided. Disposable items should not be used. Children get the notion that they, too, are disposable when paper and plastic "throwaways" are used.

Orientation
for Driving a
School Vehicle

The owner of a car knows the amount of care required to keep it in good operating condition and to minimize expensive repairs. The agency's vehicles are no exception. In fact, more care is required, since they are driven by different persons with individual driving habits, and carry youngsters who are a heavy responsibility. One must approach a school vehicle differently than one's own car. Observing a few basic principles will help keep vehicles in a safe, clean condition.

The car should not be unlocked until everyone going on the trip is grouped around the worker. When everyone is present, the following rules should be stated:

1) There is to be no smoking in the car.

2) No food is to be taken into and eaten in the car.

3) Arrangements about where children will sit for both directions of the trip must be decided before unlocking the door.

4) Seat belts and shoulder straps must be worn.

5) The rear window of a station wagon is not to be opened when the car is in motion. (Exhaust fumes are pulled into the car through the rear window.)

Safe driving demands that children behave themselves in the car. A trip is a privilege, and a "no-nonsense" attitude must be taken by the driver. Firm limits are to be set and adhered to. There is no law that says the trip cannot be canceled.

Compare the handling of a trip by the following two child care workers:

1) Mr. George takes a group of six children in the school station wagon to the ice cream parlor for sundaes. On the way, the youngsters are noisy and boisterous. Mr. George yells at them to behave themselves, without result. When they arrive at the store, Mr. George tells the children that because of their behavior in the car and because they did not mind him, they can have only ice cream cones instead of sundaes.

2) Mr. Frank takes a group of six children in the school station wagon. On the way, the youngsters are noisy and boisterous. Mr. Frank pulls the car over to the curb, has the children come out of the car and tells them that if they don't behave properly, he will turn back. The children calm down and have sundaes when they get to the store.

A final note: Any sort of accident, regardless of fault, should be reported immediately in person or in writing.

The Basics

Common-Sense Fundamentals

All that has been written in this manual boils down to a relatively few fundamentals that spell out a common-sense approach to the care of children of all ages. The basics are not new, but they certainly bear restating.

1) Never say "no" to a child when you can say "yes."

2) Everything said or done is neither the beginning nor the end, but grist for the mill of treatment.

3) Institution-type language is depersonalizing.

4) The child's unhappiness is his own. Do not take it away from him, but help him to cope with the cause of it. He will dispose of it himself.

5) The significant reduction of anger and anxiety in the child should be a major objective of every staff member in the institution.

6) Avoid acting impulsively. Good judgment is too often and too much obscured by anger and anxiety of the child care worker.

7) When you do not know what to do about a problem, go slowly. Do less rather than more.

8) Preface every decision by hearing the youngster out.

9) No child care worker has the right to be safe. Risk is an essential ingredient in any productive relationship.

10) Staff learning and self-development are treatment experiences for the children.

11) The child, on some level, gets the full message of feelings that are deep inside you, no matter what you say or do.

12) Call a child by his first name.

13) Anger begets anger, fear evokes fear. Aggression met by counteraggression produces only a perpetuation of smoldering, angry relationships.

14) Never demean the child with inappropriate demands or the unnecessary exercise of authority.

15) Do not confuse the child's needs or problems with your own.

16) Personality differences in children and staff must be acknowledged, respected and protected as inalienable rights before any judgment is made of the need to change for the sake of uniformity.

17) The child care worker's need for satisfaction must remain secondary to the child's and deferred as long as may be necessary for the child to achieve some resolution of his problem or conflict.